Pueblo Indian Cookbook

Compiled and Edited by Phyllis Hughes

Recipes from the Pueblos
of the American Southwest

museum of new mexico press

Cover Illustration:
Watercolor by Mapewe of Zia Pueblo,
from the collections of the Museum of New Mexico

Text drawings by Phyllis Hughes

Second Edition, Revised 1977

20 19 18 17 16 15 14 13 12

Copyright © 1972, 1977
Museum of New Mexico Press
Post Office Box 2087, Santa Fe, New Mexico 87503

Library of Congress Catalog Card Number: 77-76328
ISBN: 0-89013-094-9

the people

The quiet, subtle laughter of women
    as they prepare the meal.
The food, hot and steaming, nourishing,
    served in a pottery bowl; the same color as the people.
The flow of the awakening sun as it pours itself
    into the darkness of mud-plastered walls beginning another day.
This is the world of the Pueblo.

And now this is the new day:
The laughter is still subtle, still quiet.
The food is still hot, still humbly accepted and given thanks for.
Only the plaster has changed,
    but the sun is still round, like the pottery,
    like the kiva, and still the color of the people.

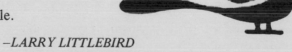

−LARRY LITTLEBIRD
Santo Domingo-Laguna

preface

The simple, wholesome foods that grow in the warm New Mexican sun are still the basis of most Pueblo Indian foods. Although at one with their past and the natural world about them, the Pueblo peoples also live in the present. Kitchens have modern stoves, electricity and other needs of the present-day cook. But there are also the outside adobe ovens, strings of red chiles, pumpkin, fruits and jerked meat drying in the clear, warm air.

Our thanks to all the gifted Pueblo cooks who shared their recipes, both traditional and inventive, with us. For much time and effort spent we especially wish to mention Juanita Gonzales, Priscilla Vigil, Damacia Coriz, Julie Herrera, Ignacia Duran and staff members of the Institute of American Indian Arts. All recipes have been kitchen tested (except Piki) using present-day cooking methods. Recipes include suggested substitutes for ingredients not always available outside of parts of the Southwest.

Thanks also to the many friends who helped with the testing and tasting.

Five years after the first appearance of this cookbook we are pleased to present an expanded edition. Many more Pueblo cooks were kind enough to tell us about and let us taste their favorites that we have here adapted from "a pinch of this and a little of that" to measurements for written recipes.

Our greatest pleasure comes with news from the Museum Press that significant cookbook sales to Pueblo Indians have thus proven its appeal to those that made this collection possible.

Phyllis Hughes
Santa Fe, New Mexico

Introduction

While recipes of the Pueblo Indians are unique, delicious and attractive, the need for Nature to provide us with the basic needs are: Rain to make the seed turn in the ground, the sun to break the earth, the air to freshen the crop and the tender care of the farmer to produce the crop.

The corn is picked, shelled and ground into flour for good atole and corn bread. Roasting ears for eating whole. Some to make chico and posoli. Yes, and we must not forget that hot stuff we call chile. We eat that raw, cooked, peeled or ground into powder if red.

Pumpkin is one of our main foods too. We fix pumpkin in different delectable ways, as a green vegetable or ripe and roasted.

Though we are educated to modern foods such as a variety of garden vegetables, fruits and store bought meat and staples, we have not gone away from our own native dishes. Many of the foods are fixed just the way our ancestors fixed them long ago.

Our Great Spirit also gave us the knowledge to know the different wild greens we eat in the spring, summer and fall. The wild berries, nuts and seeds too. We know exactly where to look for all these things.

Our thanks to Mother Nature for all the good food we get from our fields and the wild places.

Priscilla Vigil
Tesuque Pueblo

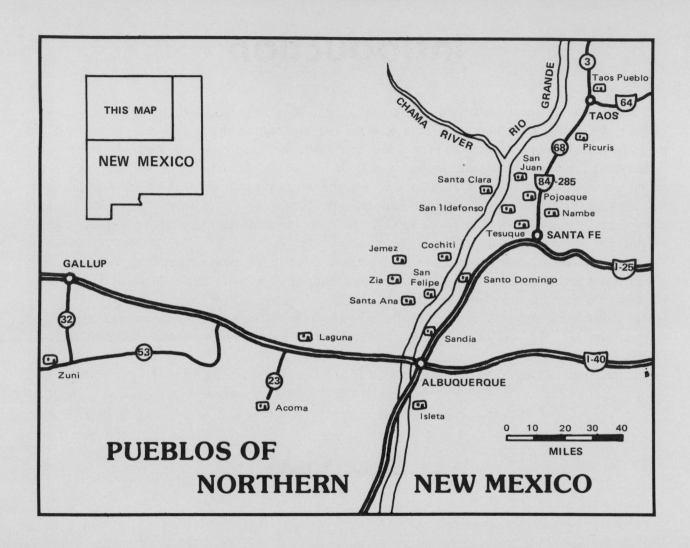

PUEBLOS OF
NORTHERN NEW MEXICO

contents

breads

The famous, crusty loaf bread of the Pueblos is still baked in the beehive shaped outdoor ovens, usually as smooth round loaves, but beautifully decorated with squash blossom and other symbolic designs for special occasions.

Corn is ground to varying degrees of fineness and used alone or with wheat flour for a variety of stove top, fried and steamed breads.

The white or blue "cornmeal" called for in some recipes is much more finely ground than regular corn meal and is always used in making corn tortillas and tamales. The white meal is made from dried lime-hominy (nixtamal) and the blue from toasted native blue corn.

Formerly all cornmeal was ground on stone metates (see cover illustration). Now this fine cornmeal is commercially produced and is called harinilla or masa harina and can be found in most Southwestern food markets and in specialty stores elsewhere.

In all baking of breads, cakes and cookies, times and temperatures may need to be adjusted according to altitude and type of oven.

Tortillas de Maiz
2 cups fine white or blue cornmeal
1½ cups warm water

Mix meal and water until dough is not sticky. Form into balls about one and three quarters inches in diameter and roll out between wax paper or pat with hands until about six inches in diameter. Cook on moderately hot dry stove lid or griddle, turning frequently until flecked with brown.

9

Pueblo Bread

9 cups flour
2 packages dry yeast
½ cup warm water
2 teaspoons salt
4 tablespoons melted lard or
 cooking oil
2 cups water

Soften yeast in warm water. Mix melted lard or oil, salt and yeast in large bowl. Alternately add flour and water, a little at a time, beating thoroughly after each addition, kneading in last of flour until dough is very smooth. Shape in ball and let rise, covered with damp cloth in large greased bowl until doubled in bulk.

Punch down, and knead on floured board for at least five minutes. Shape into four balls, put in greased baking pans, cover with cloth and let rise for 20-30 minutes in warm place.

Bake in 400° oven for 50 minutes or until tops are browned and loaves sound hollow when tapped.

Zuni Bread

1½ cups whole wheat flour
1 cup shelled, ground sunflower seeds
1 tablespoon baking powder
1 teaspoon salt
2 eggs
4 tablespoons shortening
4 tablespoons honey
1 cup milk
½ cup whole sunflower seeds

Mix together dry ingredients. Beat eggs, shortening and honey thoroughly and add to flour mixture with milk. Stir until smooth. Fold in whole seeds.

Grease bread pan and flour bottom, and spoon in batter. Bake at 350° for one hour. Cool on rack for 10 minutes in pan. Remove, but do not slice until cold.

Indian Crackers

½ cup shelled raw pinon nuts
½ cup shelled raw sunflower seeds
¼ teaspoon salt

Grind nuts and seeds together very fine, add salt and form into small balls. Flatten carefully between palms into thin wafers. Wrap each wafer in soft corn husk or aluminum foil and bake in 350° oven for 40 to 50 minutes, testing to see that crackers are not too brown. These crackers are eaten as snacks or with soup.

Filled Bread Rolls

1 yeast cake
3-4 cups flour
¼ cup warm water
¾ cup milk

2 tablespoons lard (or other
     solid shortening)
1 tablespoon sugar
½ teaspoon salt
dried peaches, apricots, apples
     small amount honey

Soak dried fruit overnight, boil until tender, chop fine and sweeten with honey. Dissolve yeast thoroughly in warm water. Mix fat, salt, sugar and milk and heat slowly until shortening is melted. Cool to lukewarm and add yeast showly. Stir in flour to make a medium dough. Cover and let rise until double in bulk. Shape into balls about three inches diameter and roll into ¼ circles.

Put spoonful of filling on one half, fold over and press top edges firmly. Grease tops of rolls, put in large, shallow greased pan, cover with cloth and let rise again to double size. Bake in hot, 400° oven until browned and crusty.

Indian Fry Bread

3 cups flour, either all white or half whole wheat.
1 1/3 cups warm water
1¼ teaspoon baking powder
½ teaspoon salt

Mix flour, baking powder and salt. Add warm water and knead until dough is soft but not sticky. Stretch and pat dough until thin. Tear off one piece at a time, poke a hole through the middle and drop into kettle of sizzling hot lard or cooking oil. Brown on both sides. Serve hot. (Sliced in two, fry bread makes delicious hamburger buns, or later toasted, very good with honey or jam.)

Fry Bread (2)

2 cups white flour
4 tablespoons powdered milk
1 teaspoon salt
1 teaspoon shortening

Combine all ingredients, add lukewarm water to make a soft dough. Pat out dough with hands until thin and shape into patty about one fourth inch thick. Fry in hot lard or other shortening about one inch deep, in large pan. Brown on both sides, serve hot with honey or jelly.

Indian Tortillas

2 cups whole wheat flour
2 cups white flour
2 teaspoons salt
4 teaspoons baking powder
1 tablespoon shortening
    (lard or margarine)
Water (or milk) to make a stiff dough

Mix all ingredients in a large pan or bowl, work in shortening thoroughly. Add liquid gradually to make a stiff dough, dry enough not to stick. Knead in pan or bowl for 5 minutes until springy. Pinch off into small balls and roll these into round flat cakes1/8" thick.Heat large iron skillet or griddle. Drop tortillas one at a time onto ungreased pan, brown on one side about 3 minutes, turn, brown other side. Put cooked tortillas between folds of clean towel. This will make 6 tortillas about 6 inches in diameter. Prepare shortly before serving with meal. They will stay warm in cloth about 15 minutes. Tortillas should be torn, not cut.

Sugar Tortillas

1½ cups white flour
1½ cups whole wheat flour
2 tablespoons sugar
1 teaspoon baking powder
1 cup warm water
¼ cup shortening

Sift dry ingredients together, work in shortening thoroughly. Add water slowly until dough is formed. Cover and let rest for 15 minutes. Divide into 10 balls and roll or pat out into thin rounds. Bake on hot griddle until done on both sides.

Sourdough Pancakes

2 cups whole wheat flour
1 cup white flour
1½ teaspoon baking powder
1 egg
1 bottle beer

Combine all ingredients and mix until smooth. Bake on hot griddle. Serve with jam, honey or syrup.

Wild Sage Bread

1 package dry yeast
1 cup native or cottage cheese
1 egg
1 tablespoon melted lard or other shortening
1 tablespoon sugar
2 teaspoons crushed dried wild sage
1 teaspoon salt
¼ teaspoon baking soda
¼ cup lukewarm water
2½ cups flour

Mix all dry ingredients together thoroughly. Dissolve yeast in lukewarm water. Beat together egg and cheese until smooth, add melted shortening and yeast.

Combine all ingredients in a large bowl adding flour mixture slowly and beating vigorously after each addition until stiff dough is formed. Cover dough with cloth and let rise in a warm place for an hour or until double in bulk. Punch dough down, knead for one minute and put into buttered pan or casserole. Cover and let rise for 40 minutes. Bake at 350° for 50 minutes. Brush top with melted shortening and sprinkle with crushed, roasted piñones or coarse salt.

Frying Pan (Blue) Bread

1½ cups flour
1½ cups blue cornmeal
    (yellow may be substituted)
6 teaspoons baking powder
1 teaspoon salt
¼ cup sugar
6 tablespoons grated cheese
¼ cup chopped sweet green pepper
¼ cup chopped onion
6 tablespoons shortening
    or cooking oil
4 teaspoons chile powder
1½ cups milk
2 eggs, slightly beaten

Sift dry ingredients, except chile powder, in large bowl. Add green pepper, onion and cheese. In heavy skillet, melt shortening or heat cooking oil, mix in chile powder. Cool, add milk and eggs. Stir mixture into dry ingredients until well blended. Return to skillet and bake in 400° oven for 35 minutes. Cut in wedges and serve hot. Eight servings.

Stove Top Corn Bread

1 cup yellow cornmeal
1 teaspoon sugar
1 teaspoon salt
½ teaspoon baking soda
1 egg
1 tablespoon bacon drippings
½ cup buttermilk
4 slices crumbled bacon (optional)

Mix dry ingredients in bowl. Beat egg and buttermilk together and stir well into cornmeal mix. Heat bacon drippings in iron skillet and pour in batter. Cover and "bake" over low heat 10 minutes. Invert on cover, slide back into skillet and "bake" ten more minutes or until center is done. Serve in wedges—hot.

Pumpkin Pinon Bread

1¾ cups cooked pumpkin
1½ cups light brown sugar (packed)

½ cup butter or other shortening, melted
3 eggs, lightly beaten
3 cups flour
2 teaspoons baking powder
1 teaspoon cinnamon
½ teaspoon each, nutmeg and salt
1 cup roasted, shelled pinon nuts

Sift flour, baking powder and spices, stir in nuts. Mix together other ingredients, and add flour mixture, blending thoroughly. Pour batter into two oiled loaf pans and bake at 350° for about one hour or until tests done. Cool on rack.

Pinon Cakes

1½ cups whole wheat flour
½ cup pinon nuts, ground to meal
2 teaspoons baking powder
¾ teaspoon salt (or to taste)
2 tablespoons sugar
2 tablespoons lard, butter or maragine
½-1 cup water

Sift flour, salt and baking powder. Add shortening and mix thoroughly. Add water a bit at a time to make medium dough.

Knead dough for 5 minutes. Cover and let stand. Pinch off dough to make egg-sized balls and roll to round cakes about 1/8" thick Bake in 350° oven or cook on stove-top griddle. Use as hot bread or serve with honey.

Corn Griddle Cakes

2/3 cup flour
1 teaspoon baking powder
½ teaspoon salt
2 teaspoons sugar
1 teaspoon finely minced onion
1 12-oz. can whole kernel corn, drained
2 eggs
¼ cup margarine, melted
½ cup milk

Combine dry ingredients. Beat eggs, add onion, corn, margarine and milk. Stir into dry mixture and drop by small spoonfuls on hot griddle. Bake 5 minutes, turn cakes and cook 5 more minutes. Makes 16 cakes.

Tortilla Bread

2¾ cups all-purpose flour
1 package dry yeast
2 cups warm water
1 tablespoon sugar
2 teaspoons salt
2 cups white cornmeal (masa harina)

Mix flour and yeast. Mix water, sugar and salt and add to flour. Stir well, then beat vigorously for 3 minutes. Stir in cornmeal and enough flour to make a stiff dough. Knead 3 to 5 minutes. Form into a ball, let rise in covered greased bowl for one hour. Punch down, let rest 10 minutes. Shape into two round loaves, and put into two greased round pans or casseroles and let rise 30 to 45 minutes. Bake at 375° for 30 minutes, remove from pans and cool on rack.

San Juan Muffins

1 cup cattail flowers or pollen (see pg. 58)
1 cup whole wheat flour
2 teaspoons baking powder
½ teaspoon salt
1 egg
4 tablespoons sunflower or vegetable oil
4 tablespoons honey
1½ cups milk
2 tablespoons toasted sunflower seeds

Mix cattail flowers or pollen and flour, baking powder and salt. Beat egg, add oil, honey and milk. Stir into dry ingredients just enough to combine the two.

Fill greased muffin pans 2/3 full and bake at 400° for 20 minutes, or until tested done.

Paper Bread (Piki)

very fine blue Indian cornmeal
1 cup of sage ashes (to preserve blue color)*
water
a brain or spinal cord from a sheep or goat

Heat five cups of water to boiling. Add four cups of very fine blue Indian cornmeal. Stir until it thickens. To the sage ashes, add enough water to make a paste, and then add two cups of hot water. Strain into about two quarts of cornmeal. This should make a dough that is stiff enough to knead. Knead well.

Add water to the thickened cornmeal dough until the mixture is about the consistency of drop batter, and mix well. Add two cups of cold water and mix again. The batter is now about like hot-cake batter, and is the right consistency for cooking.

The piki stone (a smoothly polished flat stone about the size of a serving tray) should have been heating over a wood fire for about ½ hour, and be hot enough to sizzle if water is sprinkled on it. The brain or spinal cord should be held with a cloth and passed quickly over the stone. This type of fat allows the batter to cling to the stone until it is cooked, and then it loosens easily. During a few hours of cooking, the stone may need to be re-oiled.

The thin mixture is applied to the stone by hand, very thinly. When it is cooked, it is peeled off and rolled.

*Pueblo paper bread is sometimes colored pink by addition of coxcomb or yellow with safflower.

This one recipe is included for reader interest only. Piki is fascinating and delicious but takes years of practice to develop the skill necessary to bake on a piki stone.

vegetables and chile

Corn, beans, squashes (pumpkin) and chiles predominate in Pueblo cookery. Corn especially is an ancient and most important food, closely associated with religious and ceremonial life. The Indian varieties come in a rainbow of colors and are of many kinds, some for using fresh, some for drying.

Besides the old-time crops, present-day Pueblo gardens and fields flourish with a wide choice of fresh vegetables and fruits for a variety of Pueblo dishes.

Chicos

Green corn is steamed or boiled for 30 minutes with the husks on or roasted in a slow oven for at least one hour. Test for dryness, then strip off silk and husks and hang in dry storage. Shell corn from cobs as needed. If cooked whole, kernels should be soaked overnight.

Cracked Chicos

1 cup dry corn
1 cup fresh chile sauce
2 tablespoons lard or cooking oil
1 small onion chopped
1 clove garlic, mashed (optional)
1 teaspoon salt

Crack dry corn in food grinder or with rolling pin and cook in water to cover at least one hour or until tender. Saute onion in lard or oil, add garlic if desired, drained corn, chile sauce or powder and salt. Stir in corn water until thick.

Zuni Succotash

1 tablespoon shortening
1 lb. beef, cubed small
2 cups fresh string beans, cut or 2 cups
    canned string beans
2 cups fresh corn cut from cob or canned
    whole kernel corn
2 tablespoons shelled sunflower seeds,
    crushed
water to cover
salt to taste

Brown beef well in shortening. Add vegetables and simmer until meat is tender, add crushed sunflower seeds to thicken and salt to taste. Serves three to four.

Pueblo Corn Pudding

2 cups green corn cut from cob
1 zucchini, diced fine
1 small sweet green pepper, diced fine
2 tablespoons shelled sunflower seeds or
    shelled roasted pinon nuts chopped fine

Put all ingredients in blender or mash until milky, bring to boil and simmer until thick like pudding. Serve hot with butter or chile sauce. Serves three to four.

Outdoor Corn Roast

Let wood fire die down to embers with no flames. Or glowing coals in charcoal grill. Turn back husk and strip off all silk from fresh garden corn. Replace husks and lay ears on embers. Keep turning and roast for 15-20 minutes. Strip off husks and serve hot. Corn will be taffy-colored and slightly caramelized.

San Juan Squash

3 medium yellow crooknecked squash
    or zucchini
6 slices bacon, or ½ cup chopped
    cooked carne adobado
1/3 cup finely chopped spring onions
½ cup dry bread crumbs
small amount butter or margarine
salt to taste
1 teaspoon chile powder (optional)

Slice squash in half lengthwise and scoop out seeds. Parboil for 10 minutes. Put in single layer in shallow pan, sprinkle with salt (chile powder if desired), chopped onion and bread crumbs. Top each half with bacon slice or cooked carne adobado. Bake at 350° with water just to cover bottom of pan until squash is tender and bacon is browned. Serves four to six.

Skillet Squash

5 small summer squash, cubed
1 medium onion, diced
2 roasted peeled green chiles or ½ to
    1 small can diced green chile
1 tablespoon shortening
½ cup shredded longhorn cheese

Saute onion in shortening until soft, add squash and stir until almost done. Add chiles, cook over very low fire, sprinkle over cheese and stir until cheese is melted but not stringy. Serves three or four.

Harvest Bake

2 lg. zucchini or yellow summer
    squash, sliced
1 onion, chopped
1 sweet green pepper, seeded, cut into
    thin strips
1 cup fresh corn cut from cob
2 tomatoes, sliced
1 teaspoon chile powder
1 teaspoon oregano
¼ teaspoon cumin seed
2 tablespoons grated longhorn cheese
2 tablespoons cooking oil

In iron pot (or flame-proof casserole) saute onion in 1 tablespoon oil until golden. Mix all seasonings together. Layer vegetables sprinkled with seasonings, drizzle with remaining oil. Cover and bake at 350° for one hour. Add sliced tomatoes, top with cheese and bake uncovered for 20-30 minutes until cheese is thoroughly melted and bubbly. Serves four.

Frijoles

2 cups dried pinto beans
1 medium onion, diced
4 slices salt pork, diced
water to cover beans 1 to 2 inches
salt to taste

Pick over beans and rinse thoroughly. Soak overnight in more than enough water to cover.

Put all ingredients in kettle (a dutch oven is best), cover, bring to boil and simmer until very tender. More water may need to be added during cooking.

Greens and Beans

2 bunches fresh spinach or other Spring greens
6 strips bacon or one 4"x4" square of salt pork
3 spring onions, chopped
½ teaspoon oregano
1½ cups cooked pinto (or red) beans
1 clove garlic, mashed (optional)

Fry bacon until crisp or cube salt pork and brown. Drain off fat. Put greens, chopped coarsely in same pan, add 1" water and 1 tbsp. fat and add garlic, if desired. Cook greens until almost tender (5-10 minutes).

Crumble bacon over or stir in pork cubes and cooked beans and simmer until hot.

Ignacia's Bean Salad

1 lb. cooked pinto beans (or one can)
2 cups cooked green beans
1 large sweet onion, sliced very thin
1 large sweet pepper, seeded and
    shredded
½ cup sugar
3 teaspoons salt
½ cup mild vinegar
½ cup sunflower seed oil (or other)
1 teaspoon chile powder (or black pepper)

Combine all vegetables in large bowl. Sprinkle with mixed seasonings, drizzle with oil and vinegar. Chill overnight.

Rio Corn Pie

1 cup yellow cornmeal
½ teaspoon salt
4 cups water
2 tablespoons vegetable oil
  (or melted lard)
1 bell pepper, chopped
1 medium onion, chopped
1 cup fresh corn, cut from cob,
  or one 12-oz. can whole
  kernel corn, drained
3 cups cooked frijoles, drained
2 cups cubed fresh tomatoes or
  one 16-oz. can tomatoes
3 teaspoons chile powder
1 garlic clove mashed
½ teaspoon salt
(1 cup cooked ground beef or
  sausage may be added if
  desired)
½ cup grated longhorn cheese

Mix cornmeal and salt with water and cook in saucepan over low heat for 15 minutes, stirring, until very thick.

Sauté green pepper, garlic and onion in oil. Stir in beans, tomatoes, corn (meat if desired) chile powder and salt and simmer 10 minutes.

Spread half of cooked cornmeal over bottom of casserole and top with vegetable mixture. Spread remaining cornmeal over and bake at 350° for 30 minutes. Sprinkle grated cheese on top of cornmeal and bake 20 minutes more or until cheese is bubbly.

Santa Clara Bean Loaf

4 cups cooked mashed frijoles, or
  dried limas, with ½ cup bean liquid
1 cup soft bread crumbs
½ cup sunflower seeds (or chopped nuts)
1 bell pepper, chopped
1 medium onion, minced
2 tomatoes, cubed
1 egg, beaten
1 teaspoon salt
¼ teaspoon pepper
¼ teaspoon mustard powder

Mix all ingredients thoroughly. Pack into greased loaf pan and bake at 350° for 45 minutes or until firm. Cool in pan 10 minutes, turn out loaf and slice thick. Serve with red or green chile sauce (or catsup).

21

Frijole Fry

2 cups cooked frijoles
4 tablespoons bacon drippings or lard
1 tablespoon finely chopped onion (optional)
salt to taste

Mash beans thoroughly. Heat drippings or lard in heavy skillet; add beans, mix well and cook slowly, stirring occasionally until all fat is absorbed, adding a little bean water from pot if necessary to keep beans from drying out. May be served topped with grated cheese. Serves four to six.

Leather Beans

String 4 quarts of green or yellow pole beans on heavy thread and hang on lines in a dark, dry place for two months or until thoroughly dry.

To Cook:
2 cups leather beans
water
¼ pound salt pork, slab bacon or a ham hock
salt to taste

Soak dry beans in water to cover overnight. Put beans in kettle with fresh water to cover, bring to a boil and simmer for three hours. Add pork or ham hock and more water if necessary and simmer one hour more or until just enough liquid remains to keep beans and meat juicy.

Cattail Salad

6 young stalks, 6 to 10 inches long
2 tomatoes
1 cup shredded lettuce or other
    spring greens
1 small cucumber, sliced very thin
1 tablespoon sunflower or vegetable oil
salt and pepper to taste

Peel and dice cattail shoots, cube tomatoes, and add to shredded greens and sliced cucumber. Toss with oil and seasonings.

Carrot Hash

2 pounds carrots
½ cup butter or margarine
2 teaspoons salt
1 tablespoon dark brown sugar
½ cup orange juice

Scrape carrots and grate. Melt shortening in skillet; stir in salt, sugar and carrots. Cover and cook over medium heat for 10 minutes, stirring several times. Add orange juice, cook 5 more minutes or until carrots are crisply tender.

Santa Clara Carrots

8 scrubbed carrots
3 mint leaves
2 tablespoon butter
¼ teaspoon salt

Boil unpeeled carrots with mint leaves until just tender and drain. Arrange carrots in bottom of baking pan, dot with butter, season and cover pan with foil. Bake at 350° for fifty minutes, turning once or twice. Serves three.

Baked Pumpkin

1 small pumpkin, peeled and cubed
1 cup sugar
1 teaspoon salt
cinnamon (optional)

Put pumpkin cubes in baking dish and sprinkle with sugar and salt. Cover pan with foil and bake until soft. Shake cinnamon over pumpkin.

chile

Green chiles are harvested just before they turn color and are used fresh and roasted. To roast, snip off tops and roast in a dry skillet over moderate heat. (They may also be oven roasted or baked over coals on barbeque grill.) Keep turning the chiles frequently until skin is brown on all sides and has pulled loose from the meaty part of the pepper. Cool in the same roasting pan covered with a very damp cloth. This permits peppers to steam-cool and makes peeling easy.

After peeling, they may then be chopped or mashed and with the addition of chopped raw onion, a bit of garlic, salt and small amount of olive or sunflower seed oil, a delicious sauce results.

Roasted green chiles, skinned, split and seeded, are used as a topping for fried eggs, hamburgers and grilled meats. They are an important ingredient in soups, stews, casseroles and many other Indian dishes.

Red chile is harvested in the early autumn and sun dried. The dry chiles should be washed and have stems, seeds and white veins removed unless seeds are retained for *HOT* chile. The pods are then usually made into a pulp fresh for each use. Put pods in cold water and bring to a boil, simmer for 1 hour, stirring gently. Cool, then press small end of pod and seed and pulp will slip out the cut stem end. Rub through sieve to remove any remaining seeds. Boil this pulp for 15 minutes in the water in which the pods were boiled, then salt to taste. This chile sauce (puree) is used to flavor much of the Indian cooking. The pulp from a dozen pods makes about 1 cup of sauce. One cup of sauce equals about six tablespoons of chile powder.

24

Seasoned Red Chile Sauce

1 cup chile pulp or 6 tablespoons chile powder
1 tablespoon flour
2 tablespoons lard or other shortening
1 small onion, chopped
1 clove garlic, mashed
½ teaspoon salt
pinch of wild celery or oregano

Fry onion in shortening, add seasonings, pulp or powder and flour and enough water to make a thin gravy. Stir while cooking for about twenty minutes.

Green Chile Cake

12 large chile strips
    (chiles roasted, peeled, seeded)
12 strips longhorn cheese
1 doz. eggs
2 tablespoons flour

Layer chile strips and cheese in greased shallow baking pan. Mix flour with beaten eggs and pour over. Bake in slow oven until egg mixture is firm. Cut in squares and serve hot. Serves six.

Green Chile Fry

5 green chiles, roasted
2 large tomatoes
1 onion, chopped
2 ears fresh corn
1 tablespoon lard or other shortening

Remove chile seeds, peel pods and chop coarsely. Cut kernels from corn cobs, cut tomatoes into large cubes and fry all ingredients until soft, stirring thoroughly.

Southern Rio Vegetable Chowder

1 tablespoon lard or other shortening
1 cracked beef (or mutton) shin bone
1 large onion, chopped
1 cup shredded cabbage
1 medium potato, peeled and sliced
2 small summer squash, sliced
3 beets, sliced (or three carrots)
5 cups water
2 green chile peppers chopped (or one can)
3 tablespoons dry bread crumbs

Heat water and soup bone in heavy kettle to boiling and simmer 45 minutes. Saute onion in shortening. Add vegetables to soup bone water and simmer until tender. Remove bone, stir in sauted onion, salt and bread crumbs and heat. Serves four.

Indian Mush

1 cup yellow cornmeal
1 teaspoon salt
pinch of wild sage, crumbled
½ cup green chiles, roasted,
   seeded and chopped
4 cups beef broth from soup bone

In saucepan bring 3 cups of beef broth to a boil. Mix remaining broth with cornmeal in bowl, add to boiling broth and cook over medium heat, stirring, until thick and smooth. Cover and cook over low heat, stirring from 12 to 15 minutes. Stir in green chiles and seasonings and cook 5 minutes longer.

Pack in bread loaf pans and top with wax paper or foil and chill thoroughly.

To serve, cut in half-inch thick slices, dredge with flour and fry on both sides in hot fat until brown and crusty. Very good served with fried eggs, sautéed tomato slices or cheese sauce.

Salsa Fria

4 ripe tomatoes
6 roasted green chiles
   (or 1 can chopped green chiles)
1 medium onion, minced
1 tablespoon vegetable or sunflower oil
1 teaspoon vinegar
½ teaspoon crushed leaf oregano
1 teaspoon salt
1/8 teaspoon pepper
1 clove garlic, mashed (optional)

Remove veins, skins and seeds from chiles and chop fine. Peel and chop tomatoes, add to chiles and onion. Stir in vinegar and seasonings. Let rest for at least one hour. Serve fresh.

Green Chile Relish

2 quarts chopped, peeled tomatoes
1 cup spring onions, chopped
½ cup bell pepper, chopped fine
½ cup green chile pepper, chopped fine
1¼ cups vinegar
1 cup sugar
1½ teaspoon salt
1 teaspoon mustard seed

Combine all ingredients in kettle and simmer, stirring frequently for three to four hours until thick. Cool and serve fresh or pour into hot, sterilized glasses and seal. Makes four half pint glasses.

Red or Green Chile Jelly

4 dried red chile pods or 4 roasted green chiles
1 cup vinegar
5½ cups sugar
4 sweet green peppers
1 bottle Certo or one box Sure-jell

Wash red chile pods, remove stem and seeds. Green chiles should be peeled and seeded. Grind peppers, both hot and sweet in food chopper or blender, add vinegar and sugar and boil until transparent. Remove from stove and cool for 5 minutes. Add Certo or Sure-jell and stir thoroughly. Pour into glasses and seal.

Fresh Vegetable Relish

1 cup finely shredded cabbage
¼ cup grated or finely shredded carrot
¼ cup diced tomato
¼ cup diced sweet onion
1 teaspoon salt
1/8 teaspoon dried oregano or dried
    wild celery
2 tablespoons mild vinegar
Dash chile powder
4 teaspoons sugar

Add seasonings to vegetables in bowl and pour over vinegar with enough added water to make ½ cup liquid. Mix well, cover bowl tightly and let stand overnight in very cool place or refrigerator. Serve without draining in small sauce dishes with meats.

soups

Indian cooking is slow cooking and the savory goodness of foods is brought out by long simmering. The hot, fast heat of gas or electric stoves can be slowed by the use of an asbestos mat under the soup or stew pot.

Pojoaque Cream Soup

4 cups home-cooked pinto beans
1 cup bean juice
1 clove minced garlic
1 tablespoon minced onion
¾ teaspoon salt
1 cup undiluted evaporated milk
pinch oregano
1 tablespoon red chile powder (optional)

Mash beans thoroughly and mix in bean juice or put both through blender until smooth, adding all other ingredients slowly while beating or blending. Simmer for ten minutes. Serves four.

For gourmet variation, serve cold with generous topping of sour cream.

Zuni Corn Soup

2 cups lamb or mutton
8 ears green corn
1 teaspoon salt
1 teaspoon red chile powder
6 cups water

Dice boned meat into small cubes, simmer until tender in 3 cups water. Cut corn from cob, add 3 cups boiling water and the chile powder and simmer until corn is soft.

Summer Squash Soup

3 medium size summer squash
1 clove minced garlic
1/8 teaspoon oregano
½ teaspoon salt
2 tablespoons butter or other shortening
1 cup chicken or beef broth

Dice washed squash but do not peel. Saute slowly in butter with seasonings. Keep pan covered and do not allow to brown. When soft, puree, add broth and simmer until flavors are blended. Garnish with fried squash blossoms or sprinkle of fresh raw greens. Serves three or four.

Spring Lamb Soup

1 lamb shank with meat on
1 medium onion, chopped
½ tablespoon salt
1 teaspoon coriander seed and 2 peppercorns, crushed
½ clove minced garlic (optional)
2 cups soaked pinto beans
2 quarts water

Put all ingredients in large iron kettle and simmer for four hours or until beans are very tender. Remove bone, mash beans thoroughly. Reheat. Serves four.

Pumpkin Soup

2 tablespoons margarine or butter
2 tomatoes, chopped
1 bell pepper chopped
1 small onion, chopped
1 teaspoon dried mint
½ teaspoon each, sugar and nutmeg
2 cups cooked pumpkin peeled and cubed
2 cups chicken or lamb broth
1 tablespoon flour
½ cup light cream or condensed milk
¼ cup shelled, roasted pinon nuts

Melt shortening in kettle, add tomato, green pepper, onion, seasonings and sauté 5 minutes. Add pumpkin and meat broth. Stir until blended and simmer 20 minutes. Mix flour and cream (or condensed milk) to smooth paste, stir into soup, salt to taste, heat to boiling and simmer 3 minutes.

Serve hot, with toasted pinon nuts sprinkled over. Serves four to six.

Pinon Soup

1 pound raw shelled pinon nuts
2 spring onions with tops, chopped
2 coriander seeds
1 teaspoon dried mint leaves, crushed
½ teaspoon salt
¼ teaspoon pepper
1 quart milk
1 cup water
2 cups chicken broth

Combine all ingredients and simmer, stirring frequently for ½ hour. Mash to liquid or pureé in blender. Reheat or serve cold with crumbled over corn chips.

Tortilla Soup

6 cups stock, beef or chicken
   (canned broth may be used)
1 tablespoon butter or margarine
1 large onion, minced
1 large bell pepper, chopped fine
2 tomatoes, cubed
2 small summer squash, cubed
2 tablespoons lard or oil
8 tortillas

Sauté onion and bell pepper in shortening, add tomatoes and squash, cook 5 minutes, add to stock in kettle. Bring to boil and simmer 30 minutes.

Cut tortillas in narrow strips and drop in sizzling lard or oil, stir once and drain on paper towels. Add these tortilla "noodles" to soup when ready to serve.

Chick Pea (Garbanzo) Soup

½ pound dry chick peas
¼ pound salt pork
1 small onion, minced
1 clove garlic, mashed
1 pint water
1 pint meat stock (or canned broth)
salt and pepper to taste

Cover chick peas with salted warm water and soak overnight. Drain, add remaining ingredients, water and broth. Cover and cook 1½ hours or until chick peas are tender.

Bolitas (Round Bean Soup)

¾ cup dry round beans
¾ cup diced potato
¾ cup cooked or canned tomato
1/3 cup shredded fresh, or diced canned green chile
2 tablespoons lard, bacon drippings or other
    shortening
1½ teaspoons flour
1½ teaspoons salt
1½ cups milk

Cover beans with water and soak overnight. Add salt, more water and simmer until fairly soft, but do not boil, as this destroys flavor. When almost done, add potato and onion, cook thirty minutes, adding water if needed. Mix flour with shortening, add tomato and green chile and stir into bean mixture. Simmer ten minutes, add milk, reheat and serve for four.

Garden Soup

3 cubed small summer squash
1 cup green beans, sliced
1 cup tiny peas in pod or shelled peas
1 soup bone with meat (lamb or beef)
6 cups water
1 onion, sliced
1 green chile pod chopped or 1 tablespoon
    red chile powder
1 teaspoon dry mint or fresh leaves, chopped

Cook soup bone in water in kettle one hour or more. Remove bone, add remaining ingredients, cook 15 minutes, add mint and salt, stir and serve.

stews and dumplings

White Corn Hominy

1 quart dry white corn kernels
2 quarts water
½ cup slacked lime (available at builders
    supply firms)

Dissolve lime in water in large kettle. Add corn and stir well. Boil for 30 minutes or until hulls loosen. Let stand 30 minutes then wash thoroughly in cold water, working with hands until dark tips of kernels are removed. Rinse again until water is clear. (Always used for Posoli.)

Posoli

2 cups posoli corn (lime hominy)
6 cups water
1 lb. pigs feet, beef tripe, cubed pork or
2 lbs. pork ribs
½ lb. pork rind
4 red chile pods made into unseasoned sauce
    (see chile sauce recipe) or
3 tablespoons red chile powder
1 tablespoon chopped onion
1 clove garlic, mashed (optional)
2 teaspoons salt (or to taste)
2 teaspoons oregano

Cook posoli corn in water to cover until kernels pop. Add red chile sauce or powder, meat and pork rind. Bring to boil in covered kettle, adding water to cover as needed and simmer until meat is very well cooked and corn is tender, at least four hours at low temperature. Day long cooking at lowest simmer temperature improves flavor even more. Cut meat from bones and add chopped onion and seasonings. (Green chiles, roasted and chopped may be substituted for red.) Simmer covered for an additional thirty minutes. Serves four to six.

Chile Stew with Corn Dumplings

3 cups water (or more as wanted)
2½ cups diced peeled potatoes
2 cups cooked pinto or other
    dried beans
2 teaspoons salt
1 tablespoon lard or other shortening
1 large onion, chopped
1 lb. ground beef or lamb
3 large fresh tomatoes or one
    number 303 can tomatoes
2 teaspoons chile powder or
    1/3 cup red chile pulp.

Mix first four ingredients in good-sized kettle. Saute onion in melted shortening. Add beef and cook until meat loses red color. Add chile powder and tomatoes, stir thoroughly and add to first mixture. Bring to boil and simmer for 30 minutes. Drop dumpling mixture by heaping tablespoonfuls on top of stew, cover and simmer 8-10 minutes.

Corn Dumplings

1 cup flour
1 teaspoon baking powder
3 tablespoons cornmeal
1 cup fresh corn from cob
    (or canned whole kernel corn)
Salt to taste

Mash corn thoroughly or grate in blender. Mix all ingredients until well blended. Add water if necessary but keep dough fairly stiff.

Juniper Lamb Stew

2 lbs. lean lamb, cubed small
6 ears fresh corn
6 spring onions with tops, chopped
3 sweet green peppers, chopped
1 tablespoon flour
2 tablespoons lard or cooking oil
2 teaspoons dried wild celery (1/3 cup chopped
    celery tops may be substituted)
1½ teaspoons salt
5 dried juniper berries, crushed
2 teaspoons chile powder
4 cups water

Mix seasonings and flour to coat meat and brown in hot lard or oil in heavy kettle. Cut corn from cobs and add with other ingredients and water to meat. Cover and simmer for one hour or until meat is tender. Serves four.

Hopi Corn Stew

1 cup ground goat meat (or ground beef)
2 cups green corn cut from cobs
1 small sweet green pepper, chopped
1 cup summer squash, cubed
salt to taste
1 tablespoon whole wheat flour

Fry meat in a little fat (shortening of any kind) until brown. Add rest of ingredients and cover with water. Simmer until vegetables are almost tender. Stir 2 tablespoons cooking water with 1 tablespoon whole wheat flour, return to cook pot, simmer five more minutes while stirring. Add blue corn meal dumplings if desired.

Blue Corn Dumplings (with stew)

1 cup harinilla-blue corn meal ground to flour
2 teaspoons baking powder
1 teaspoon bacon drippings, lard, or other
    shortening
1/3-1/2 cup milk
1 teaspoon salt

Mix (or sift) dry ingredients thoroughly, cut in fat and add enough milk to make drop batter. Drop by spoonfuls on top of stew.

Cover kettle and steam dumplings 15 minutes before lifting cover. Stew should be kept bubbling. Serves four to six.

Green or Red Chile Dumplings for Beef or Lamb Stew

1 cup whole wheat flour
1 cup white flour
2 teaspoons baking powder
¼ cup lard (or other shortening)
¾ cup milk
½ cup finely chopped fresh roasted green
    chiles (or 2 tablespoons chile powder)
1 teaspoon salt
pinch oregano

Mix (or sift) flour, baking powder and salt together. Cut in shortening. Add milk, enough to make a soft dough. Add green or red chile, oregano and mix thoroughly, add a bit more milk if necessary. Drop by large spoonfuls on stew. Cover and simmer 15 minutes. Serves six.

Squash Blossom Stew

5 large squash blossoms
3 summer squash, cubed
1 cup sliced green beans
1½ lbs. lamb or beef, cubed small
3 ears fresh corn
3 spring onions with tops
1 clove garlic mashed
2 teaspoons salt
½ teaspoon oregano or 3 mint leaves
8 cups water

Boil meat until tender, remove from stock. Cut corn from cob, chop spring onions and add all vegetables to stock and simmer until just tender. Add meat seasonings and squash blossoms, simmer 15 minutes. Serves four to six.

Green Tomato Stew

1 pound ground beef
1 medium onion, chopped
4 ears green corn
2 large zucchini or yellow
    summer squash
4 medium green tomatoes
6 pods fresh green chiles
2 teaspoons cooking oil

Brown beef in oil. Add chopped onion and shredded chiles and saute five minutes. Add cubed squash, sliced tomatoes and corn cut from cob.

Simmer over low flame for 30 minutes. Season to taste. Serves three.

Indian Spaghetti Stew

3 roasted green chile pods, chopped, or one small
    can chopped green chiles
1 pound ground beef
1 cup corn cut from kernel (or whole kernel
    canned corn)
1 medium onion, chopped fine
2 large fresh tomatoes, sliced
2 mint leaves or pinch of oregano
1 small package long spaghetti
water

Brown beef and onion thoroughly, add corn, green chile, tomatoes and water to cover. Simmer until corn is almost tender. Break spaghetti into inch pieces and add to stew, adding enough more water to cook spaghetti. Cook ten more minutes. Serves four.

meats

Green Chile Bake (Menudo Verde)

1 lb. tripe
2 tablespoons bacon drippings or other
    shortening
1 large onion, chopped fine
3 peeled white potatoes
1 can chopped green chiles
2 tomatoes, sliced or 1 small can tomatoes

Wash tripe in cold water, cover with water and simmer for three hours. Drain and cut into strips. Slice potatoes very thin, add onions, tripe and chiles and brown in skillet in hot fat. Cover skillet and bake at 325° for 40 minutes. Serves three or four.

Green Corn Tamales

1 dozen ears fresh white corn in husks
1 cup pure lard
1½ tablespoon salt
1 lb. ea. boiling beef and pork, cooked until tender
½ tablespoon cooking oil
1 clove garlic, crushed
3 tablespoons red chile powder
1½ cups meat broth
1 teaspoon oregano

Remove corn husks, wash and soak briefly, spread to dry. Slice corn from cobs, chop fine or put in blender until like fine textured mush. Blend lard and salt, add mush and ¾ cup meat broth and mix thoroughly.

Chop meat fine and fry in cooking oil. Add all seasonings and rest of broth and cook until thick. Wash and soak large corn husks for a few minutes, dry and spread flat. Spread each ¼ inch thick with mush mixture. Put 1 tablespoon meat mixture in center of dough, fold sides of husk together, bring top and bottom to center and tie with corn husk strips. Put in wire basket in large pot over boiling water and steam for 45 minutes. Makes about three dozen tamales.

Feast Day Pork Roast

4 lb. pork roast—loin or
    boneless butt
2 cups tomato puree
½ cup raisins
1 teaspoon chile powder or ¼ cup
    unseasoned red chile sauce
½ cup chopped sweet pepper
1 tablespoon onion, chopped
1 clove garlic, mashed
1 teaspoon dried sage
1 teaspoon oregano
2 teaspoons salt
1/3 cup flour

Mix all seasonings except chile and rub into roast. Place fat side up in pan and roast at 350° for 2½-3 hours. Reduce temperature to 250°. Pour off drippings into skillet, add onion and green pepper and saute. Thicken drippings with flour, add chile powder to sauce, tomato puree and raisins, add water if too thick and simmer for 10 minutes. Return roast to pan, drizzle with sauce and roast for 30 minutes, basting two or three times with sauce. Serves six to eight.

Spiced Pork (Carne Adobado)

2 cups red chile puree made fresh from
    24 dried pods or 12 tablespoons
    chile powder
3 pounds fresh, lean pork
2 teaspoons salt
1 tablespoon oregano
1 clove garlic, mashed

Cut pork into strips about 6x2x2 inches. Mix all other ingredients and add to pork strips and let stand in cool place for 24 hours. Cut as much meat as is needed for one meal into cubes and brown in small amounts of fat. Add chile sauce and simmer one hour or more. This meat may be dried and used later. To dry, thread strips taken from chile sauce and hang in the shade to dry. After thoroughly dry, store in a cool dry place. To prepare dried meat, pound until well shredded with back of cleaver or side of metal lid. Add fresh chile sauce and cook until tender.

Jackrabbit Stew

1 jackrabbit (or domestic hare or
    5 lb. baking chicken)
1 large onion, chopped
1 teaspoon salt
2/3 tablespoon chile powder (optional)
1½ cups flour
2 quarts water
2 large onions
6 large carrots, halved
2 sweet peppers, halved and seeded
4 teaspoons salt
2 cups cooked lime hominy
¾ cup melted lard or cooking oil

Cut rabbit (or other) into serving size pieces. Dredge in flour. Put oil in large kettle and heat until sizzling. Brown all pieces of meat on all sides, drain and pour off excess oil. Return meat to kettle, add water and simmer for two hours, add all vegetables and simmer until carrots are tender.

Taos Rabbit

1 rabbit
2 quarts cold water
1 cup mild vinegar
2-3 teaspoons red chile powder
1 large onion
1 teaspoon salt

Cut rabbit into serving pieces, peel onion and put all ingredients into stew pot and simmer until meat is tender. Thicken gravy with flour or ground sunflower seeds. Serves four.

Green Chile Balls
(Served as a dessert for weddings and Feast Day)

2 lbs. pork boiled until well done
2 lbs. boiled beef
3 cans chopped green chiles or 1 dozen roasted
    green chiles, peeled and chopped fine
½ cup sugar
½ cup raisins
2 eggs
½ cup flour
2/3 cup shortening
2 sweet onions, chopped fine

Cool meat, put through grinder. Fry onions, add meat, chiles, raisins and sugar, mix thoroughly. Cool mixture. Separate egg yolks and whites. Beat whites until very stiff, fold in beaten yolks, and spoon into a shallow dish. With a little of the flour in one hand, shape meat-chile mixture into small, egg-shaped balls. Roll in egg mixture until thoroughly covered, lift gently with spoon and slip into fat heated to sizzling in kettle. Keep turning gently until golden brown. Drain on paper.

Red Chile with Meat

1½ lbs. lean chuck beef, cubed
½ cup chile pulp or 3 tablespoons
    chile powder
2 tablespoons lard or other
    shortening
1 teaspoon salt
1 teaspoon oregano
1 clove garlic, mashed
3 large ripe tomatoes
    (or one no. 303 can)

Boil meat until tender. Fry in shortening until browned. Add chile pulp or powdered chile and stir in seasonings. Add tomatoes. Cook for thirty minutes.

Marrow Bone Butter

2 or 3 beef marrow bones
    (shin bones)
Dash salt and pepper

Crack bones and roast in 350° oven for one hour or until marrow feels soft when tested.

Have toast or tortillas ready, scoop out marrow and serve hot on breads, after seasoning to taste.

Beef Jerky

(Easy to make and great for hikers, campers, hunters and kids)

Cut a chunk of lean (no fat) boneless beef into 4-inch squares. With a very sharp knife slice with the grain of the meat, starting at one end, into ¼ inch strips, unrolling into one long piece (see diagram*). Take each strip by its two ends and stretch (actually jerk). Then thread with string by one end and hang strips, not touching, on line. If hung in the hot sun during the day and protected from any dampness at night, the meat will dry in a few days. Jerky may also be dried indoors in a warm, dry place with good air circulation.

Jerky is good for munching, as is, or cut into squares, may be cooked in soups and stews, or soaked until soft and fried with onions and chile.

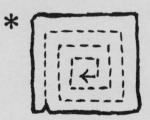

Cured Venison

3 pounds salt
4 tablespoons cinnamon
5 tablespoons black pepper
4 tablespoons allspice
fresh solid chunks of venison

Cut meat into strips 12 inches long, 2 inches thick and 4 wide. Remove all membrane so curing mixture will adhere to moist meat.

Mix dry ingredients together thoroughly and rub well into every surface of strips, dusting on more. Thread each strip on string and hang them in dry cool place out of sun, not near artificial heat. Needs to be hung for a month then is ready for eating without cooking.

Venison Pemmican

4 pounds cured venison
1½ pounds fresh raw animal fat
1 cup dried apricots or dried
    wild plums

Cut fat into small chunks and try out in skillet until melted. Grind jerky fine and pour hot fat over. Mix until the consistency of sausage. Chop dried fruit finely and add. Pack pemmican in plastic or other airtight container, after shaping into small balls or rolls.

Venison Steak

1 inch thick venison round steak
    (beef may be substituted)
1 small can tomatoes
1 onion chopped
4 teaspoons flour
½ teaspoon chile powder
¼ teaspoon salt
2 teaspoons lard or other shortening

Mix flour, chile powder and salt and dredge steak thoroughly. Fry onion in shortening, add steak and brown well on both sides. Add tomatoes and enough water to cover. Simmer in covered pan 50 minutes or until tender.

Campfire Jerky

6 to 8 strips jerky
1 teaspoon lard or suet
1 large onion
3 medium potatoes
1 can pie cherries, drained *or*
1 handful chokecherries, freshly gathered

Put jerky and fat in iron pot, cover with water and cook until meat is plump and tender. Cut meat in chunks, add onion, potatoes, cherries (or berries), salt to taste, and simmer until vegetables are done.

Roast Leg of Mutton

4 pound leg of mutton
2 tablespoons lard or other shortening
2 teaspoons salt
1 teaspoon dried mint leaves, crumbled
1 teaspoon pepper
1 clove garlic, crushed
1 medium onion, sliced
2 cups fresh or canned tomatoes
5 medium carrots, scraped
5 celery stalks (or 1 bunch wild celery)

Mix shortening, garlic and seasonings, coat mutton leg well on all sides with mixture. Roast uncovered at 400° for 30 minutes. Add vegetables, cover and bake at 350° until meat tests done as desired.

Juan's Beef Ribs

3 pounds beef short ribs
1 tablespoon shortening
1 teaspoon salt
1 clove garlic, crushed
1 large onion sliced
2 cups canned tomatoes (with juice)
1 large roasted green chile, peeled and chopped
    (or 1 small can green chiles)

Season ribs with garlic and salt; brown well in melted shortening in pot. Drain off excess fat, add onion, and just cover ribs with water. Simmer, covered for two hours. Add tomatoes and simmer for 30 minutes more. Serves four to six.

Taos Beaver Tail Roast

1 or two beaver tails
salt and pepper to taste

Broil tails over hot fire or under broiler until rough hide peels off easily. Roast tail meat in moderate oven until fork-tender. Delicious served with refried beans or garbanzo soup.

Wild Turkey Roast

(Domestic fowl may be substituted)
1 eight pound wild turkey
1 cup melted butter or margarine
1 teaspoon salt
½ teaspoon pepper
1 recipe pinon nut stuffing

Rub cavity of oven-ready turkey with salt and pepper. Fill loosely with pinon stuffing, truss and brush with ½ cup melted shortening. Roast at 350° for three to four hours, basting often with remaining ½ cup melted shortening.

Pinon Nut Stuffing

4 cups coarse dry bread crumbs
   (Pueblo bread preferred)
2 cups shelled, roasted pinon nuts
1 medium onion, chopped
1 beaten egg
1/3 cup melted butter or margarine
1 teaspoon salt
½ teaspoon pepper
½ teaspoon wild sage leaves, crumbled

Melt shortening in skillet, add onion and sauté 5 minutes, add crumbs, seasonings, egg and pinon nuts. Toss to mix thoroughly.

Isleta Beef (or Lamb) Roll

1½ pounds ground beef (or lamb)
1½ teaspoon salt
1/8 teaspoon pepper
1 garlic bud, mashed
1 medium onion, chopped
2/3 cup milk
1 roasted green chile, peeled, seeded and chopped
   (or 1 small can chopped green chiles)
½ cup crushed corn chips or toasted tortillas,
   ground to fine crumbs
1½ cups fresh corn cut from cob, or 12-oz.
   can whole kernel corn
¼ cup catsup

Mix together beef, crumbs, onion, milk and seasonings. Pat or roll out to 12-inch square.

Combine corn and green chile. Spread over meat and roll to a cylinder, sealing edge and ends. Place on rack in uncovered pan and bake at 350° for ½ hour. Brush all sides with catsup and bake ½ hour more. Serves five to six.

desserts

Brown 2 cups sugar slowly in skillet until caramelized. Add water slowly to make a thin syrup. In deep baking pan or casserole, layer bread, cheese, raisins and 1 cup sugar. Sprinkle with cinnamon and pour boiling syrup over. Bake in slow 300° oven until all liquid is absorbed and pudding is dark brown but soft. Let stand for ½ hour before serving. Serves four to six.

Feast Day Cookies

2 cups whole wheat flour
4 cups white flour
2 teaspoons baking powder
1 teaspoon salt
2 cups lard
1½ cups sugar
¾-1 cup water
1 cup shelled pinon nuts

Mix dry ingredients thoroughly. In another bowl, blend shortening and sugar until fluffy. Gradually add flour to this mix. Gradually add water until non-sticky dough is formed. Add pinon nuts. Roll out on lightly floured board until ½ inch thick. Cut into fancy shapes and dip into a mixture of sugar and cinnamon. Bake in 375°-400° oven until crisp.

Nambe Governor's Pudding

1 loaf white bread, sliced and
    toasted dry
½ lb. longhorn cheese, sliced thin
1 cup raisins
3 cups sugar
cinnamon to taste
vanilla if desired

Sprouted Wheat Pudding

4 cups sprouted wheat meal
2 cups whole wheat flour
8 cups boiling water
1½ cups sugar
3 tablespoons butter

Mix wheat meal and flour thoroughly. Add boiling water to make a thick paste, cover and let stand.

Caramelize sugar, add 1 cup boiling water and stir to make syrup. Pour over wheat mixture in heavy pot or casserole and bake in outdoor oven overnight or in slow stove oven until thick and dark brown. Very good served warm with cream.

Fry Bread Pudding

6 pieces Indian fry bread
1 cup sugar
1 cup water
½ cup raisins
1 teaspoon cinnamon (optional)
1 cup grated mild cheese

Split fry bread into thin halves. Caramelize sugar, add water to make syrup. Layer fry bread, raisins and cheese. Pour syrup over mixture and bake in 300° oven until all syrup is absorbed.

Little Pie Filling

Many different dried fruits are used in Indian pies: peaches, apricots, wild plums, prunes and raisins.

2 cups dried fruit, cooked and drained
1 cup sugar
1 teaspoon cinnamon

Chop fruit finely or beat to mush. Add sugar and spice and stir.

Little Fruit Pies

1½ cup flour
6 tablespoons shortening
1 teaspoon baking powder
½ teaspoon salt
4 to 6 tablespoons water

Mix flour, baking powder and salt. Cut in shortening until like fine meal. Add water slowly until dough is easy to roll. Roll out to 1/8 inch thickness. Cut in rounds about four inches in diameter. Put heaping tablespoon of fruit filling in center of each pastry round, top with another round and pinch edges together scallop fashion. Decorate top with pricked design. Bake at 400° until lightly browned.

Pueblo Peach Crisp

¾ cup white flour
¾ cup brown sugar
½ cup butter or lard
¼ cup granulated sugar
¼ teaspoon salt
6 fresh peaches, peeled and sliced

Cut peaches into ¾ inch slices or small cubes (makes 5-6 cups). Mix granulated sugar and salt and sprinkle over each layer of peaches as spread in shallow pan. Combine flour and sugar in bowl and cut in butter until size of peas. (Chopped roasted pinones may be added.) Sprinkle mixture evenly over peaches. Bake in 375° oven for 45 minutes or until topping is crumbly and brown. Serve warm with cream or whipped topping. Serves six-eight.

Isleta Rice Pudding

3 tablespoons raw rice
1 tablespoon sugar
1 quart milk
½ teaspoon salt
½ teaspoon cinnamon
2 eggs
½ cup raisins or ½ cup
    soaked dried apricots

Wash rice, add all other ingredients except eggs. Separate eggs, beat whites until very stiff. Add beaten yolks and fold into rice mixture. Spoon into baking pot or casserole. Bake in slow 250°-300° oven for two hours, stirring several times.

Tortugas
½ cup lard
1½ cups white masa harina
1/3 cup dark brown sugar
½ teaspoon salt
¾ teaspoon baking powder

Whip lard and sugar until fluffy. Mix in masa, baking powder, salt and water. Spread each heaping tablespoonful of dough on a flat, soaked corn husk, 3½″ x 5″ (cooking parchment may be substituted). Smooth dough to a 3½″ x 2½″ rectangle, put one teaspoonful of sweet filling in center and fold according to diagram.

Put tortugas with folded sides down on rack in steamer and steam 45 to 60 minutes. Test for doneness by opening one husk (or wrapping). Masa should be firm and not at all sticky. Best served hot.

Sweet Filling
¼ cup butter or margarine
1 cup dark brown sugar
½ cup toasted piñon nuts
¼ cup chopped raisins

Blend shortening and sugar. Stir in nuts and raisins.

Pumpkin Candy

1 five pound pumpkin
5 cups sugar
1 tablespoon baking soda
water

Peel and seed pumpkin, cut in 2″ x 4″ strips. Stir baking soda into enough water to cover strips and let stand 12 hours then drain and wash strips in running water. Drop pumpkin into pot of boiling water and cook until tender but not soft. Remove and crisp in ice cold water and drain. Mix sugar with one cup water and boil 10 minutes. Add pumpkin and simmer in covered pot until syrup is thick and strips are brittle. Spread strips to dry. May be stored when cold.

Indian Corn Pudding

½ cup yellow cornmeal
½ teaspoon salt
4 cups milk
2 tablespoons honey
6 tablespoons dark brown sugar
1 scant teaspoon cinnamon
½ cup raisins

Heat milk to scalding. Mix cornmeal and salt and stir slowly into hot milk until smooth. Add honey-sugar mixture, stir in raisins and cinnamon. Bake at 300° for 1¾ hours. Serve hot with cream.

drinks

Tiswin

5 pounds dried white corn
2 gallons water
1½ cups brown sugar
2 dried orange peelings
3 cinnamon sticks
1 teaspoon ground cloves

Oven-roast corn at 300° until light brown, stirring frequently. Grind coarsely in food chopper or in small quantities in blender. Wash in several waters and discard hulls.

Put in crock and stir in water and other ingredients. Cover and let sit in a barely warm place for five or six days or until fermented. Strain through cheesecloth and serve.

Elder Blossom Wine

1 quart stemmed blossoms
3 gallons cold water
5 pounds sugar
1 yeast cake
3 pounds raisins

Wash blossoms thoroughly. Add water and sugar and ferment mixture in crock with yeast cake. Let stand nine days. Strain and add raisins.

Store in covered crock in a cool dark place for six months. Decant and bottle. Wine will be a pale yellow.

Elderberry Wine

5 pounds elderberries
1 gallon cold water
3½ pounds granulated sugar
½ ounce yeast
6 cloves
½ teaspoon ginger

Wash berries well, cook in kettle with gallon of water until fruit is tender then strain off juice into crock. Add sugar and spices, stir thoroughly and when lukewarm, add yeast. Cover crock, store in cool place for 10 days then strain and bottle. Put away for six months.

Chackewe (Atole)

1 cup blue cornmeal
1 quart boiling water
salt to taste

Stir cornmeal into water, little by little. Serve as a gruel with milk. If boiled until thick with a little lard or butter added it may be chilled, sliced, fried and served with chile sauce.

Pinole (Hot Corn Drink)

2 cups blue or white cornmeal
½ cup sugar
½ teaspoon cinnamon
milk

Brown the cornmeal in a hot 425° oven for 8-10 minutes by spreading in a thin layer on a cookie sheet, stirring several times to prevent scorching. Add sugar and cinnamon and use like cocoa in about the same proportions stirred into hot milk and simmered for 15 minutes.

Corn Maiden of the Hopis

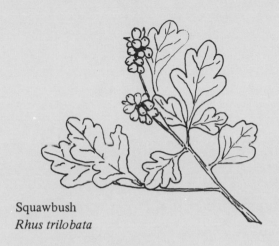

Squawbush
Rhus trilobata

Squawbush Lemonade

Squawbush berries should be gathered in September before they begin to dry.

½ cup berries
1 quart water
sugar to taste

Tie berries in porous cloth and boil in water for 10 to 15 minutes, mashing fruit twice. Add sugar to taste and cool. Pour off "lemonade" from any sediment in bottom of pot.

Indian Tea
(Sometimes called "Navajo Tea")

Gather *cota* plants, breaking each stem off above the roots, and tie each plant in a small bundle (see sketch). Plants can be gathered before or during flowering and may be used fresh or sun-dried.

Put bundle of fresh or dried tea in small pot of boiling water and steep 4 to 5 minutes. Very good with a little honey.

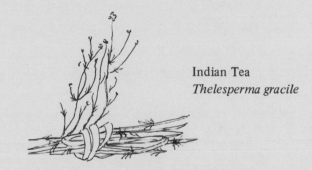

Indian Tea
Thelesperma gracile

Sunflower Coffee

Save hulls of sunflower seeds when shelling. Brown hulls in skillet, stirring to prevent burning. Grind hulls fine and steep in boiling water for three minutes, allowing 2 teaspoons per cup.

wild foods

The gifts of Nature are shared but not despoiled by Pueblo people who since prehistoric times have found healing and nourishment in the seeds, fruits, leaves and roots of wild plants. They are knowledgeable harvesters of wild foods, but to many urbanized people edible and poisonous plants are difficult to tell apart. Here therefore are a few recipes for plants that are safe to gather.

Pinon Pine
Pinus edulis

Common Sunflower
Helianthus annuus

Pinon Nuts and Sunflower Seeds

The pinon, or pine nut, has always been an important source of Southwestern Indian food. Families go gathering in the fall, shaking ripe nuts from cones in the trees, gathering those that have fallen. Pinones used to be roasted slowly over an open fire, then stored for winter eating.

These sweet, rich nuts are used in many ways: cracked singly and eaten as snacks, shelled and baked in cookies, cakes and pies and ground into meal to be used as thickening for stews and gravy or mixed with other flours for baking.

Sunflower seeds, so rich a source of vitamins and minerals, have been widely used by Indians since prehistoric times, parched and eaten whole or ground into flour. These seeds, put through a grinder, may be mixed with flour or cornmeal for mush, bread making or soups. The ground seeds are also boiled until the oil rises to the surface and can be skimmed off for use as an excellent cooking oil. Seeds of both wild and cultivated flowers are used.

To Roast Pinones

May either be roasted in a hot 425° oven for ten minutes, stirring frequently, or spread in a flat pan and roasted at 250° for 1 hour, shaking pan occasionally. To shell, put between damp cloths while still hot and roll vigorously.

To Roast Sunflower Seeds

Roast in 250° oven for no more than one hour. Test for doneness. To shuck while still hot, put between damp towels and roll lightly.

Pinon Nut Gravy
2 cups shelled pinon nuts
water to cover
salt to taste

Crush pinons, boil until oil rises to top, skim, boil again and season with salt.

Curly Dock
4 cups early spring leaves
½ cup water
tablespoon vinegar or squeeze of lemon
salt and pepper to taste
crumbled crisp bacon optional

Boil leaves for 10 minutes, add seasonings. Young leaves may be used raw in salads.

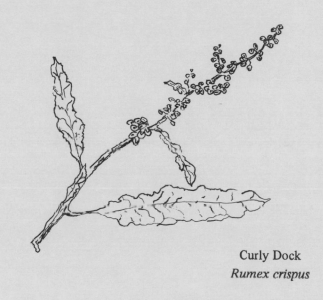

Curly Dock
Rumex crispus

Lambs Quarter (Quelites)

4 cups tender tops of plants
1 onion, chopped
4 slices bacon, fried crisp
¼ cup vinegar
¼ teaspoon salt

Saute onion in bacon fat, add vinegar and salt and bring to simmer. Add washed greens and stir just until they become limp. Sprinkle crumbled bacon over and serve hot. Serves 2-3.

Lambs Quarter
Chenopodium berlandieri

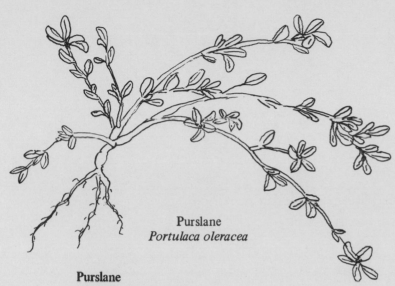

Purslane
Portulaca oleracea

Wild Mustard

Young leaves and the yellow flowers are used raw in salads. Tender shoots with leaves are cooked in boiling water, covered, about 20 minutes. Usually mixed with other more bland greens.

Ripening mustard pods are gathered and spread out on cloth to dry, then beaten to release the seeds which are then ground and used as a seasoning or mixed with water and a bit of vinegar to a paste and used as a spread.

Purslane

4 slices bacon
2 medium onions, chopped
2 medium size tomatoes
1 clove garlic, mashed
3 cups purslane leaves
salt to taste

Cook bacon until crisp and drain. Saute onion in bacon fat, add all other ingredients except purslane and cook 15 minutes. Add purslane and crumbled bacon, stir for one minute until greens are limp. Serves two or three.

Wild Mustard
Brassica nigra

Plantain—Indian Wheat

4 cups tender young plantain leaves
    (no stems)
1/3 cup boiling water
salt to taste—(crumbled crisp bacon
    optional)
Cook covered for 2-3 minutes.

Plantain leaves may be dipped in milk then in flour and fried over low heat for 30 minutes. Good hot or served cold like chips.

Wild Celery
Phellopterus

Steamed Wild Celery

6 cups small, tender wild
    celery greens
2 spring onions, chopped
1 tablespoon bacon drippings
salt to taste

Wash greens thoroughly in two or three (cold) waters, having removed all roots. Spread in baking pan, add sprinkle of water, onion and drippings, cover pan with foil or tight-fitting lid and let steam in a slow oven for 20-30 minutes.

May be dried and used in stews or sprinkled on roasts or chops.

Plantain
Plantago major

56

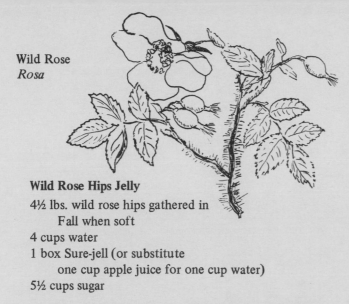

Wild Rose
Rosa

Wild Rose Hips Jelly

4½ lbs. wild rose hips gathered in
    Fall when soft
4 cups water
1 box Sure-jell (or substitute
    one cup apple juice for one cup water)
5½ cups sugar

Remove blossom ends of hips, split and remove balls of seeds. Crush fruits thoroughly, add water, bring to boil and simmer, covered for 10 minutes. Pour into cloth bag in large bowl, tie top of bag and hang over bowl until all juice has drained from bag. This should yield about 4 cups juice.

Mix Sure-jell (or apple juice) with rose juice in large saucepan and bring to hard boil over high heat. Add sugar and bring to rolling boil for one minute stirring constantly. Remove from heat, skim, pour into sterilized glasses and seal.

Yucca Sweets

Ripe fruits of the broad-leaved yucca are gathered and baked in a covered pit overnight—now sometimes baked in a slow oven for several hours—until skins can be peeled and the ball of seeds and fiber removed. The residue is a sweet paste which is used as a filling for pies and turnovers or shaped into bars and sun-dried or slow-oven dried to make delicious candy.

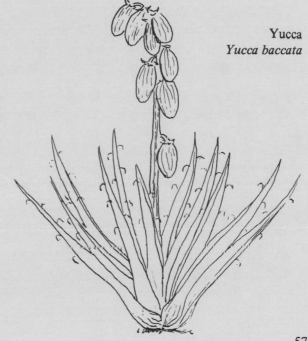

Yucca
Yucca baccata

Prickly Pear
Opuntia spp.

Prickly Pear Jelly

Pick fruit with tongs when red-ripe. Roll in sand or brush under running water to remove some of the small spines (glocids). Put in kettle with water to cover and boil 15 to 20 minutes.

Drain water and mash fruit thoroughly. Line mesh strainer with doubled cheesecloth and strain pulp, letting strained juice stand to settle sediment. Pour off juice carefully to avoid sediment.

3½ cups clear juice
1 package powdered pectin
½ cup lemon juice
4½ cups sugar

Mix juice and pectin in pan, bring to a boil stirring constantly. Add sugar and lemon juice and boil hard for 3 minutes. Remove from heat, stir and skim. Pour into sterilized glasses and seal. Makes about six glasses.

Cattails
Typha angustifolia

Cattail Flour

Strip pollen-producing flowers from upper part of cattail stalks in summer. Spread in single layer on cookie sheet and roast in 350° oven until completely dry, stirring often to prevent burning. Cool and store in dry, closed containers.

Use mixed with wheat flour for pancakes, muffins, cakes and cookies.

Later in the season when pollen begins to shed, the flower heads may be shaken over a sheet of wrapping paper. When a considerable quantity of this yellow dust has collected, sieve carefully to remove insects and chaff. Use with flour for baking and pancakes.

this and that

To Sprout Wheat

Wash untreated wheat grains, drain but do not dry. Spread in a single layer in shallow pans and cover with damp cloths or put wet seeds in a cloth bag. Keep dampened in a warm dark place. When sprouted, if wheat is to be ground, dry thoroughly before putting in grinder or blender.

Dried Fruits and Squashes

Sun-dried fruits and melon strips were and are a welcome addition to winter meals and supply vitamins as well as flavorful fillings for pies and turnovers.

For those who live in a sunny climate, it is most rewarding to dry your own fruits.

Pueblo peoples gather wild plums to dry and use the peaches, apricots and apples from their orchards as well as melons and squashes from their gardens. For melons and squashes, shave off rind with a sharp knife, cut in half and scrape out all pulp and seeds. Hang halves to dry in sun for a day. (A cheesecloth covering will protect all drying fruit from flies.) Cut melons and squashes spirally in long strips and hang on a line in the sun. Peaches, apricots and plums are split, stoned and spread on screening in the sun. Apples are cored, cut into thin rings and hung on string to dry.

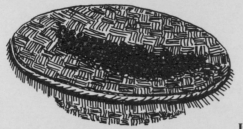

Squash Blossoms

2 doz. squash blossoms
2/3 cup milk
1 scant tablespoon flour
½ teaspoon salt
½ cup cooking oil

Pick large squash blossoms in early morning just before they open.

Thoroughly mix milk, flour and salt. Spread blossoms in large, shallow pan and gently spoon flour mixture over to coat all sides.

Heat oil in heavy skillet to french-fry temperature. With slotted spoon carefully put batter-coated blossoms in hot oil until they turn golden brown. Drain on paper toweling and serve hot as fritters or as garnish for soup.

Indian Cheese

1 quart sweet milk
1 rennet tablet
salt to taste

Crush rennet tablet to powder and dissolve in two tablespoons of milk.

Heat remaining milk to lukewarm. Stir in rennet, remove from heat and let stand in warm place until mixture thickens. Break curd, put into thick cheesecloth bag and hang over bowl until all whey has drained off. Season and chill. Makes one cup.

Toasted Squash Seeds

Stir some fine wood ash in water and soak seeds in this for six hours. Husks are then easily removed. Toast seeds with butter or oil and salt in 250° oven, stirring occasionally until done to taste.

Pinon Chips

3 cups flour
1½ teaspoon salt
1½ cups shortening
½ cup (more or less) water
½ cup butter
½ cup chopped pinon nuts
1 teaspoon milk

Sift flour and salt and cut in shortening. Add water just to hold flour mixture together. Roll out ¼ inch thick and spread with softened butter. Fold pastry over three times one way, turn and fold three times again. Chill. Cut in half and roll each half about 1/8 inch thick. Cut into one inch squares. Brush with milk and sprinkle with nuts. Bake in 450° oven for 10 minutes until light brown. Makes eight dozen.

Chick Pea Spread

(For corn chips, tostados or crackers)
4 cups cooked chick peas *or*
1 16 oz. can chick peas
2 tablespoons olive, vegetable or
    sunflower seed oil
3 tablespoons lemon juice
3 tablespoons very soft cheese
    (Indian cheese if possible)
½ cup chopped, seeded green chiles
2 tablespoons chopped, roasted pinon nuts
    (or other nuts)

Drain chick peas, stir in all other ingredients except nuts, and mash then whip or whirl in small quantities in blender until smooth. Garnish with chopped nuts.

Fruit Honey

12 ounces dried apricots or peaches
2½ cups water
2 cups sugar

Combine all ingredients in saucepan. Bring to full boil, reduce heat and simmer 50 minutes. Mash until well blended or purée in blender. Serve with Indian bread or toast.

Fruit Rolls

Peaches, pears or apricots may be used. Wash fruits and pit or seed. Quarter and put in blender or mash and whip to a smooth paste to make 3 cups of purée.

Spread puree in cookie sheets, smoothing with spoon to an even ¼ inch thick. Dry in hot 80° sun for 8 to 10 hours or on shelf in warm place for one to two weeks. (Pans may be covered with protective cheesecloth after the first three hours. For oven drying, put in 120° to 150° oven, leaving door slightly ajar for steam to escape.

In any method, dry purée until very firm and edges can be lifted easily. Peel fruit sheets from pan while warm and roll into scrolls. Put in paper or cloth bags to continue drying for four to five days.

Fruit rolls should remain pliable and may be stored in airtight containers for quite some time . . . if not discovered by small Indians!

index